GW00381388

The Real Secret to Winning on the Horses

Published by Steve Wharton

Wolviston, TS22 5LP, England

ISBN 9798360822370

Copyright © stevewharton2022

A CIP record is available for this book from the British Library

The moral right of the author has been asserted

Printed in Great Britain by Steve Wharton

Contents

Introduction

Welcome to **'The Real Secret to Winning on The Horses',** the first book in the new series specifically created for Amazon Kindle priced at £1 UK and 1$ US in kindle format and £3.99 or $3.99 in paperback. The books fit into the kindle short book category of around 7000 to 10,000 words equating to approximately a 45 minute read and I sincerely believe this format and price represents excellent value for money.

The books offer a unique viewpoint by assessing the particular subject matter through the powerful lens of 'High vibrational thinking', which brings a fresh and empowering perspective. This enables the reader to access new avenues of approach in terms of utilising and benefitting from the information presented. In other words, **'secrets are revealed'**.

Please do not be deterred by the relatively short length of the book because if anything this adds to the clarity and simplicity without losing any of the important content.

I do feel that sometimes writers can unnecessarily over complicate things when trying to pad out a book, which in turn can detract from the essence and value of the work.

In this instance and indeed in this series of books simplicity is paramount in order to give the reader the best possible opportunity of effectively capitalising on the work. Also when you have read and digested the information this should facilitate a shift in your thinking process, which then allows your mind to see new and exciting possibilities.

Integral to this is a basic but clear understanding of how your mind works, an essential component in empowering you to be able to make important internal changes and as high vibrational thinking brings a relatively simplified perspective to this, it should help you to comfortably and successfully make those changes.

Chapter one gives a brief explanation of how we live in a world which is in fact in its most basic form energy, this understanding and view is essential in order for you to be able to really digest and benefit from the information contained in the rest of the book. Then I relate this to the subject matter covered, in this instance 'winning on the horses', which is finally followed by a technique or practice which you can easily use when needed allowing you to put into action what you have learned.

So off we go and I hope you have an informative and enjoyable read and please believe me what you are about to read **really does work**. So soak it all up, maybe read it a few times to make sure it sinks in and triggers the paradigm shift in your thinking that you are about to experience and of course, enjoy your winnings.

I should also mention that I have for over thirty years worked in various forms of the gambling industry, which includes time spent as a manager for one of the UK's biggest bookmakers. So I have vast experience in observing what winning looks and feels like, it's something that I understand and have been around for a long time.

I have also referenced various esteemed works in respect of quantum physics and recommended appropriate books regarding some of the key points that I talk about, should you feel the need to look further into what you may consider the more challenging aspects of this book. I encourage you to explore these avenues as the more information from different sources that you process, the more sure you will

—

become of the sincerity of this work and in turn the more confident you will be when picking your winners.

The biggest hurdle you have to overcome to take advantage of what you are about to read is shifting your old programmed view of how life actually works. And if we can achieve this, you will open the door not only to knowing how to back winners but also to changing your life in many other positive ways.

I believe this truly offers you an opportunity to become not just a winner on the race track but also in many other aspect of your life.

And please check out my list at the end of the book for other forthcoming titles available in 'The Real Secret' short book series.

Chapter 1

Energy

'If you want to find the secrets of the Universe, think in terms of energy, frequency and vibration'.
-Dr Nicola Tesla

The first thing I would like you to understand is that you live in a world that is in fact pure energy. Yes that's right everything you see around you including your physical body is actually made from energy, which in its basic form is atoms, microscopic atoms that are pulsing and vibrating.

The house you live in, the car you drive, trees, furniture, food, animals etc are all made up from these tiny atoms, any scientist or physicist will confirm this. So if you are made from energy (atoms) and as science tells us all energy is vibrating then at some level you must be vibrating?

This is correct; you are constantly vibrating even though you can't directly sense this happening, although you are aware of when your mood fluctuates from high to low or to put it another way, when you go from feeling happy to sad, this is when your vibration is shifting from fast to slow.

This vibration shifting happens all the time as you encounter the ups and downs of everyday life. This is you sensing your energy vibration, through the way that you feel.

And as I said when you feel good you are vibrating fast and when you feel bad your energy vibration is slowing down.

That makes sense because fast vibrating feelings are joy, excitement, happiness, peacefulness, serenity and love etc and slow vibrating feelings are anger, fear, anxiety, depression, jealousy, greed, hate etc.

So the spectrum range of feelings goes from fast vibrating 'love' down to slow vibrating 'fear' with all the variations in between.

Now you can see how our world of energy works and why everyday of your life you experience many different positive and negative feelings as you ride up and down on the vibrational roller coaster ride we call life. It's a muti-vibrational energy experience in every sense of the word.

As Deepak Chopra says the universe is energy and information.

"The whole universe, in its essential nature, is the movement of energy and information."

-Deepak Chopra, The Seven Spiritual Laws of Success: A Practical Guide to the Fulfillment of Your Dreams

This is what High Vibrational Thinking is all about, knowing how it works from an energy point of view and then using that information to help you to stay in as high a vibration as possible every day of your life.

Dr Shawna Freshwater explains our world of energy and vibrations further.

What is Vibrational Frequency of Emotions?

'First, let us understand that every cell in your body has the vibration of life whether you are aware of it or not. Every cell is compromised of energy and your potential of fully resonating with Life Force. Every cell in your body is affected by the emotional vibrational frequency that you manifest.

Second, Emotions have voltage. The vibrational frequencies of emotions are on a

vertical dimension of contraction and expansion relative to the vibrational voltage of a particular emotion.

Emotions resonate with the vibrational frequency that they generate. The higher the vibrational frequency, then the higher the expansion, and the greater the Life Force in your cells. The lower the vibrational frequency, then the greater the contraction, and the lesser of Life Force in your cells.

-Dr. Shawna Freshwater, PhD licensed Clinical Psychologist, Neuropsychologist, and Holistic Practitioner.

Chapter 2

How it works

'Since everything is a reflection of our minds, everything can be changed by our minds'.
-Buddha

Now that you know everything is energy and on a personal level the faster you are vibrating the better you feel, it makes sense to consider this fact, that the better you feel, the easier it is for you to successfully pick winners in horse races or indeed win in any other form of gambling and this is because when you are in the higher vibrations (the feeling good place) you are existing where there is much less negative energy around.

So therefore intentionally raising your vibration and putting yourself into a happier state of mind will greatly increase your chances of winning on the horses. The happier you feel the more you will win and this is not just because you are in the higher vibrations (although that does play an important role) but also because you personally have much more influence than you realise on the outcome of a race.

And it's much easier for that to be a positive influence rather than a negative influence when you are in a high vibrational place with less negative energy around because you will have less of it tugging and niggling away at you.

The other side of the coin is when your vibration is low and you are experiencing feelings such as unhappiness, anxiety, stress, worry, anger, frustration, depression etc you are more likely to experience losing because you are existing where lots more negative energy is present, so it can more easily seep in and infect your thoughts, feelings, emotions and beliefs.

So the unhappier you feel the more you will lose because the influence that you have on the race will be more tainted by negativity.

Doubts, lack of belief, feelings of anxiety, stress, worry etc are much more prevalent in the lower vibrations, so if you exist in a lower vibrational state of mind or are temporarily feeling negative for whatever reason, you are much more likely to have those negative types of thoughts, feelings and emotions. They exist there, they are swirling all around you and the negative energy that you are carrying inside of you (we all have some of this it's often called trapped emotions or your inner demons) will have more control over you and this source of internal negativity will influence and infect you spilling out and messing with whatever is happening on the outside.

"Negative experiences lower our personal vibrations and we feel bad. This state attracts more negative experiences leading to negative vibrations. Lower vibes are bad for health of the soul."

-Hina Hashmi, Your Life A Practical Guide to Happiness Peace and Fulfilment**.**

Remember that your experiences reflect back to you where your vibration is, so if you are in a lower more negative vibration you will in general have experiences that are in harmony with that, experiences that invoke feelings such as disappointment, failure and losing, this is 'normal' in that range of vibration. Success is not easy to come by when you are here.

To clarify, when you are in the high vibrations you may feel energised, full of fun and laughter, joyful, excited, happy etc, these are the active feelings of being in the higher vibrations. Or you may feel serene, tranquil, totally calm and have a sense of inner peace; these are the more relaxed feelings and moods of being in the higher vibrations. And either way this is the best vibrational place to be, if you are to back winners.

In the lower vibrations you may feel angry, frustrated, stressed, worried, irritated etc, these are the active feelings of the lower vibrations. Or you may feel depressed, somber, unhappy, deflated, low etc, these are the more subtle negative moods of the lower vibrations and not the place to be if you are to back winners.

Okay so we know you can feel up or down but how can this possibly mean that our mood could have any effect on the outcome of a horse race?

'Everything is energy and that's all there is to it. Match the frequency of the reality you want and you cannot help but get that reality. It can be no other way'.
-Albert Einstein

How you feel influences the race because you are in fact living in a belief driven reality where your beliefs have a massive impact on a particular horse race that you may be interested in and everything else in your life that you do, or are involved in. You are instrumental in which horse wins through what you believe, in other words you are creating the reality you experience through your thoughts, feelings, emotions and ultimately your beliefs. As Einstein says '*Match the frequency of the reality you want and you cannot help but get that reality*'.

The next chapter details an actual day when by pure chance the energies came together and I believed, which created an amazing experience for myself, this will help you to understand how it can work.

And without doubt you will have had days like this yourself so hopefully this will explain and help you understand more clearly what took place.

Chapter 3

Grand National Day

I must share an experience I had one day when I first realised how powerful believing and creating the right energy was in respect of influencing the outcome of a horse race.

It was Grand National day here in the UK 2009, the biggest race of the year and as I had worked in the industry I had come to the conclusion, through many years behind the counter, that, as the odds favoured the bookmaker it may not be prudent to bet, so I never normally bothered.

However I was having breakfast with my daughter and we were in a jovial mood and as I looked through the daily newspaper I realised it was Grand National day, so I said to her 'let's have a bet, just for a bit of fun' and we had no idea whatsoever who was running nor anything else about the race. I had lost touch with the racing scene as I had left that particular job years before.

I made my choice by choosing the name of the horse because it resonated with me, it was called 'My Will' I had no idea who was riding it, what the odds were, who the trainer was or anything else, it was purely a selection based on the name, it stood out somehow.

Next it was my daughter's choice, well she wasn't really interested and said to me, 'you choose', I said 'no you have to do it, I tell you what take your pen and close your eyes and let the pen drop on the paper and we will take the horse it lands on'. 'Okay,' she said. So she did this and the pen dropped onto a horse called Mon Mome, a 100/1 outsider.

Our bets were placed £5 each way (paid for by me of course) and later on that day we settled down to watch the race. Neither of us at this point was even thinking about winning; we were just having a fun enjoyable day together with no serious concern about the race whatsoever, we had our pizza and nibbles and were comfortable on the couch.

Soon the race was off and in typical Grand National style they were bunched and hurtling over the fences with fallers here and there. As the race progressed I remember saying 'oh look both of our horses are still in the running'. Well this created an excitement in the air as we both started shouting at the TV for our respective horses and it was at this point more to do with surprise and having a little banter between ourselves than anything else.

It's worth pointing out here that we were having great fun cheering the horses on but we were coming from a place of zero expectations and had absolutely no thoughts about feeling disappointed should our horses fall away, in our minds the fact that we were still in the race and somewhere near the front was a success, you could say we were already embodying the mindset of having won. In fact it was a small miracle still being in the race given it was the Grand National as not many ever finish the race, just doing that was something of a victory and that's how it felt, like we had already won.

At this point the excitement and joy increased and bounced around the room with the dog adding to it by running around barking as we shouted at the TV. As the race came to the last few furlongs we were still in with a shout and the excitement reached fever pitch. The energy was now really strong and palpable as we excitedly kept cheering and our fun approach took on a real extra surge as we realised that we were in with a chance to actually win the race.

This was the point when it seemed comfortable to consider the fact that one of us may well have the winner. Our energy was in such a good place (happy, excited, joyful, and full of fun) that it was not a stretch at all from here to believe we could win. And sure enough the horses crossed the line with my daughter's horse winning and mine coming third. It was incredible she won £635 and I won £15 not a bad return for what started out as a daft fun bet just for a bit of interest.

It was some years later that I realised what had really taken place that day. The high energy that we had produced through our excited fun filled day had as the race progressed powerfully drawn that race into our reality. The excitement, laughter and joy had virtually carried our horses to victory (or ensured we had a very positive result) and we had no negative energy involved because we had nothing emotionally invested in the prospect of not winning. In other words, had we not won, we wouldn't have felt disappointment because our selections had already done so well and it had all started out as a fun bet simply for a bit of interest.

Like I said, because of the way that we had chosen the horses (for a bit of fun without any assessment of form, jockey, weight, going etc), just finishing the race felt like a victory, it felt like a great achievement. We had nothing invested in our choices, it was all done from the energy of joy, if we lost it did not reflect or hurt us one bit.

Unlike when you study the form and use your expertise and best judgment to pick the winner and when it loses you were wrong, which can easily trigger disappointment, feelings of failure and frustration.

The less you have invested yourself in your choice, the less chance of stirring up negativity when things don't go according to plan.

From an energy point of view the less effort you put in when choosing your horse, the less vulnerable you are when it looks like it might not go your way. And this means the less damage you will sustain vibrationally and that's good if you are going to place more bets, as well as ensuring more than likely a better result in that race.

I now believe the energy that we created throughout the race built up our belief levels and got our horses into a great position approaching the final few furlongs and then we had no problem shifting from this happy, excited, having fun mindset to actually believing we could then win the race as the finishing line approached.

Our high vibrational energy powerfully attracted to us the result that we wanted and we had held this high frequency happy mood over the course of the race.

In a nutshell we won because we were not taking it too seriously, which had we done so could easily have allowed in negative energy through stress, anxiety, fear etc, increasing the likelihood of us experiencing a different outcome.

Not becoming emotionally triggered if you lose is a vital part of the equation of winning.

Have fun and keep it that way is the lesson, win or lose.

Chapter 4

Matching the reality

Now back to how matching the frequency of the reality you want gives you that reality. The vortex of energy that you are at the subatomic level consists of atoms, protons and neutrons, which are constantly vibrating and this generates your unique vibrational signature, created by what you have become through your many experiences in life.

This means your distinctive perspective and beliefs are constantly pulsing out into the Universe and this is what draws to you the people, places and events of your life.

"You are already a VIP - a vibrational interference pattern. Your vibration is as specific and unique to you as your fingerprint."

-Catherine Carrigan, Unlimited Intuition NOW

Remember like energy attracts like energy.

So become the frequency of winning, harmonise with the feeling of winning, then this feeling will become part of your vibrational signature and you will pulse this out into the universe and that is what you will get because you will have matched the frequency.

As Einstein said '*match the frequency and that's what you will get*'. If you really and truly believe you will win, or can get yourself into the feeling of having already won then this means you have matched that vibration so that is what you will get.

'The law of life is the law of belief'
-Joseph Murphy

Joseph Denis Murphy was an Irish author and New Thought minister, ordained in Divine Science and Religious Science and author of 'The Power of your Subconscious Mind'

You are creating it all, win or lose you are instrumental in what happens through the vibrations you send out.

And most of the time you don't know what vibrations you are sending out, as much of it comes from the subconscious level of your mind. This means at any given moment you probably don't really know exactly what you believe.

Your best clue to this is how you feel, this gives you an insight to what your vibration is at any given moment and that can indicate where your beliefs are about any given thing.

'Man moves in a world that is nothing more or less than his consciousness objectified'
-Neville Goddard

Neville Lancelot Goddard, generally known as Neville Goddard, was a Barbadian New Thought author and mystic who wrote on the Bible, esotericism and is considered to be one of the pioneers of the law of assumption.

Your consciousness creates your life via your vibrational signature which is constantly pulsing out from you.

If you believe 100% that the horse you have picked will win, **then it will win**, and you will have a feeling of certainty about the outcome. If you don't believe 100% and don't have the feeling of certainty, the best way to give yourself that feeling is to put yourself in the mindset that you would be in, if the race was over and your horse had already won.

As Neville Goddard said, the secret is to **'Assume the feeling of the wish**

fulfilled'. This means you must fast forward to the state you would be in had your horse just won the race. Embody the state of mind and the energy you would be feeling, had the wish already been fulfilled.

Another way Neville describes this is **'Feel the fulfillment of your desire and dwell in the state of it having already taken place'.** Training yourself to conjure up the feelings of having already won and allowing them to wash through your mind and body is the secret. As Neville says **'feeling is the secret'**.

Matching the frequency of what you want by feeling like you have it, is the secret to getting it.

If you can successfully train yourself to assume the state of having already won, then you will have successfully attained 100% belief that your horse has indeed won the race and you will be having all the feelings associated with that outcome, joy, happiness, relief, excitement, fulfillment, success and a knowingness, a feeling of certainty that you won. So you will know you have managed to attain the correct state when you are having these positive types of feelings, this is your barometer. And you can become proficient at doing this because just like any skill the more you practice the better you get.

—

So back to you creating the outcome through your beliefs, essentially every possibility can happen because we live in a Universe which contains every probable outcome or to look at it another way, every horse wins the race, you just choose the race that you will experience through what you believe.

And you can deliberately select the outcome you want by adjusting your beliefs and this is done by tweaking your feelings to that of your horse having already won.

When you successfully do this you match the frequency of the reality where your horse wins and this is what you draw into your experience, it can be no other way.

'One of the most exciting and enticing topics to speculate about is the idea that our reality — our Universe the way it is and the way we experience it — might not be the only version of events out there.

Perhaps there are other Universes, perhaps even with different versions of ourselves, different histories and alternate outcomes, than our own.

When it comes to physics, this is one of the most exciting possibilities of all.'

-Forbes -Forbes Magazine

If there are eight runners there are eight different winners and you tune into the particular race that you believe in the most, this draws that reality to you and that becomes your experience. As Neville says you must change the inside to change the outside.

'Your world is your consciousness objectified. Waste no time trying to change the outside; change the within or the impression; and the without or expression will take care of itself'.
-Neville Goddard

Exactly what you believe is not something that you would be particularly aware of because most of your innermost beliefs are held at the subconscious level. Again your best indicator of what you really believe is by gauging how you feel.

Learning to control and alter your feelings is the secret to shifting your beliefs. You can be the master of this world by training yourself to control your feelings and visualisation is the way that you can practice this skill.

If you don't believe 100% that your horse will win then you may sense this as feeling a little apprehensive, slightly worried, only hopeful, mildly doubtful etc. Your lack of complete 100% belief has left the door open just a bit for negative energy to creep in and boy will it creep in.

This of course is the mindset of just about everyone that is betting on the race, so in general everyone is infected by various levels of doubt to some degree and this means if you don't employ a strategy to get your head in the right place you have very little chance of winning consistently.

This is why it is so difficult for you to pick winners; in your natural normal walking about (full of doubts) state, it is very hard for you to believe 100% that you can on a regular basis pick the winner.

This is when you will more than likely find random thoughts flickering up in your mind containing potential reasons why your horse may not be the winner and these thoughts will seemingly float up out of nowhere.

It's like the negative thoughts are swarming and buzzing around your head, just like a swarm of flies, some strong clear and powerful buzzing in your ear and others barely perceptible but still faintly there just in the background.

And some you will not so much hear but sense as feelings like a mild flutter of dread or an uncomfortable shimmer of anxiety moving through you.

What if he falls?
What if he gets boxed in?
What if the ground is too soft?
What if I lose?
What if he doesn't try?
The other horse looks good?
Etc..........

Of course you have probably studied the form and weighed up the pros and cons when making your selection. So you pick your horse based on all the information you have available and you place your bet. This is how it usually works but it would be very rare if ever that you would assess the race and this would work you up to believing 100% that your horse would win the race. Probably more like 60% to 70% at best presuming you have backed the favourite, even less for outsiders. This still leaves the door open for the swarm of negative thoughts always ready to pounce and infect and dilute your level of belief. So as the race is running you are buzzed by the negative thoughts hovering around your head. This can easily change the possible outcome mid-stream as you are bombarded with various different feelings created by what you are seeing happen in the race or by what you are hearing from other punters, TV commentators etc.

Eventually the race is over and you experience whatever you believed in the most, though I doubt you will have any real clue as to what that was. The trick is to get control by learning to sense your feelings and tweaking them as and when needed and this will mean you have more influence on the outcome of the race.

Your feelings need to be your focus during the race, this is what you should be paying attention to even more than what's happening in the race.

So if you can put all your efforts into making yourself believe 100%, by concentrating on your feelings you will be amazed at how the swarm of flies dissipates or even disappears.

This is the secret, you must concentrate your conscious mind on something positive as my daughter and I had done accidentally on Grand National day and learn to completely ignore the swarm of negative thoughts that usually hover around. Give yourself a positive focus and force yourself to think of that or you can visualise something serene and peaceful and focus on that, either way you focus your conscious attention on something positive and high vibrational during your day at the races, especially during the race.

Your feelings are something you must be aware of all day and even more intensely during the race because if you let your guard down sure enough the flies will be back buzzing around your head messing with your beliefs and feelings and therefore messing with your chances of winning.

Learning to hold the correct state of mind is vital and key to your success.

This is the training you must do, discipline yourself to be able to attain the feelings and the knowingness that you have already won and then hold those feelings when the race is in progress no matter what your eyes see taking place.

The simple fact is that you are creating your own reality as you go along and I know this may be difficult to understand but this is how it works. Without getting too deep into it and running the risk of over complicating things I ask you for the moment just to accept the fact that we all are existing in our own version of reality and we are creating it through what we believe. You are drawing it to you as you go along.

*'Hugh Everett devised **the many-worlds interpretation of quantum mechanics**, in which quantum effects spawn countless branches of the universe with different events occurring in each'.*

-Scientificamerica.com Hugh Everett III was an American physicist who first proposed the many-worlds interpretation of quantum physics, which he termed his "relative state" formulation.

And as our beliefs waver we get different results, 100% belief in something creates exactly that but when doubt is in the air other outcomes can and do happen and this is usually the case. I could write a whole book on this subject alone (creating your reality haphazardly) but in the interests of keeping it simple in this book I will leave that for another day.

However if you are interested in learning more and would like to do your own research I have included a list of excellent books and articles at the end that will confirm what I am saying and answer all of your questions.

If you allow a shimmer of negativity in it will open the floodgates for doubt to enter the equation and it will come at you from every angle: Is he the best jockey? Is he carrying too much weight? Is his form good? What going suits him best? I can't afford to lose! And so on.

When doubts are flickering through your mind you are really in a minefield of endless possibilities and this makes picking the winner (or choosing the race you will experience in your reality) much more difficult. So why not detach from all of that and work on drowning out all the negative thoughts by convincing yourself that the horse you have chosen **HAS ALREADY WON,** this is a much better approach and will pay dividends if you can practice and master it.

You must concentrate on nothing but believing your horse has won, forget all the potential reasons why it might not; you must close the door on all negative based thoughts. And remember all the horses win the race, you are choosing the race that you **will experience** by strongly focussing on the **feelings** that your horse has already won and this will draw that race into your reality.

As soon as you realise this is how it works, your ability to create your reality will move up to another level. And remember many of the greatest minds now and in history have been telling us that we create our own reality, Jesus, Buddha, Neville Goddard, Albert Einstein, Wayne Dyer, Joseph Murphy, Nikola Tesla, Deepak Chopra, Louise Hay, Rhonda Byrne to name a few.

'Jesus said unto him, if thou canst believe, all things are possible to him that believeth'.

-Mark 9:23 King James Bible

Of course many people will still not be able to understand or believe that this could be true, even with that list of names confirming it. So they will dismiss it completely thereby rendering themselves unable to take advantage of this opportunity. **However believe me this is the secret and training yourself to believe your horse has already won is how it's done.**

'You are given the gifts of the Gods; you create your reality according to your beliefs. Yours is the creative energy that makes your world. There are no limitations to the self except those you believe in'

-Seth 'The Nature of Personal Reality

So if you are still with me and want to know more, keep reading.

In the interests of attaining 100% belief and being able to hold that thought pattern initially it makes sense to place only small bets that will not cause you too much concern if you lose, especially while you are practicing attaining the skill. This will help to keep the negativity at bay, for example it would be much more likely that you would feel stressed and anxious (negative) if you gambled your house on a race therefore keeping it sensible and under your anxiety threshold will help you to be able to hold the belief that your horse has already won.

This will eliminate one avenue of attack that negative thoughts normally come through.

And don't forget your barometer is the way you are feeling, the happier you are the better, so make it fun. This is how you know you are mentally in the right vibrational place, you need to be overjoyed that your horse has won and you are experiencing all the good feelings associated with that.

This is your focus, **'feeling good'** don't worry about what is going on in the race, simply keep your mind focussed on the belief that you have won and holding the feeling of joy is all that matters.

And of course practice makes perfect so keep repeating this over and over and you will see through the success you will be having that **something incredible is happening** and it's not about your skill at picking winners or your amazing knowledge of horse racing, it's about **FEELING GOOD**, this is how you win and you can play around with this for as long as you want to hone your skills.

Try picking favourites and notice how this makes you feel, then try picking outsiders to see if this feels different. Is there more negative energy clawing at you, not forgetting it doesn't matter which horse you pick because they all win. Obviously outsiders will potentially create more doubts especially at first but it's a good measure of where you are in terms of mastering the skill.

And keep the bets small and affordable especially while you are practicing and maybe turn the sound down on the TV to minimise outside input.

Of course you will have had winners before when unbeknown to you the energies aligned and you were vibrationally in the right place even though you may not have been aware of it. It's even possible that you may have felt down and unhappy and still had winners but you could be unhappy and still believe enough. However, now your ability to back winners will improve dramatically because you now have an understanding of what is happening and you have a method to follow based on that understanding. You are no longer cast adrift in a sea of choppy emotions.

So let's look at the key points to be aware of to help you attain and hold 100% belief that your horse has won the race, therefore enabling you to generate the good feelings associated with that outcome.

Bet amounts that you can afford. (Most important in the early days although you should never bet amounts that trigger your anxiety threshold).

Have a mini-visualisation and mantra that you can use to focus your conscious attention during the race. Maybe repeat something like the following mantra over and over in your mind '**YES, my horse has won the race'**, this will help drown out and keep at bay the negative doubts that may be hovering around. And you could accompany this mantra with a mini movie of your horse surging into the lead as they cross the finish line (see 3 steps coming shortly).

It's probably best not to tell anybody what you are doing as this could create doubt from them (because they don't understand the process) and this could then generate negative energy from them or trigger it from within yourself, which could easily drag down your vibration making it more difficult to get into the 100% belief mode needed. Of course this doesn't mean you can't talk to your friends about it later but its sensible not to discuss it when you are in the middle of using it, in case their initial reaction is negative.

It's very important to try to hold yourself in a high vibrational state such as happy, joyful, excited, ecstatic, serene, peaceful, tranquil etc, as this will help keep you in the best feeling place to have winners. This is why it is so beneficial to 'assume the feelings of the wish fulfilled' because this automatically puts you in a high vibrational place as well as in harmony with the feelings you would be having had your horse already won.

This is why people often experience success when it's their birthday or they are on holiday or their son or daughter has been born etc, or maybe some other special occasion and this is because they are in a happy mood; they are already in a good feeling place.

And as you now know it's a lot easier to move into true 100% belief mode when you are already in the higher vibrations.

It doesn't matter if you lose (something that will always happen even when you have mastered this and are having many more winners) and this is an important part of the process, you must not be bothered if you lose because if it does bother you, you will be allowing floods of negative energy in and this will drag you down the vibrations.

When you let in disappointment, anger, frustration etc you are plummeting down to a vibrational place where it will be much more difficult for you to climb back up to the lofty vibrations of feeling that you have already won.

You must feel **NOTHING** if you lose and this will keep you at as high a vibration as possible and therefore make it easier for you to be able to attain the belief 100% that your horse has won in the next race.

You must be unphased no matter what happens.

This is an essential part of the discipline of winning, training yourself to feel nothing if you lose is paramount to your overall success; you must give losing no energy.

This is because when you are emotionally invested in losing you are seeping in negativity, you must feel content and happy even if you lose. Detachment is the key and you must be aware of this at all times.

Just see a loss as a necessary step bringing you closer to the next great result; it is simply part of the process.

It is an inevitable experience even to the most skilled practitioner of the art of believing.

Chapter 5

Recap

If you can hold yourself in a high vibrational state when you place a bet and train yourself to hold that state of mind you will win more and you will win even more if you can train yourself to attain the feelings of having already won.

It's all about creating the right vibration conducive to winning. It must be filled with joy, fun, laughter, excitement or the calmer side of the higher vibrations inner peace, tranquillity and serenity. This will lift you up the vibrations and hold you there increasing your chances of winning and make it easier for you to get into the mindset of believing you have already won.

Negative vibrations anger, frustration, worry, stress, tension, anxiety, fear and doubts will drag down your vibration putting you in a vibrational place where you increase the chances of losing. And it's very difficult to make yourself truly believe when you are in the lower vibrations; you are surrounded by and bombarded by so much negative energy.

I think lots of people experienced winning on the lottery when it first started.

Ten pounds here and even thirty pounds there was quite common, at first. Then it dried up and somehow you rarely seem to even get those small wins anymore.

This is because at first in respect of the lottery you were in a higher vibrational state than you are normally. Everybody got caught up in the initial excitement and **positive thoughts and energy** of maybe winning the lottery.

We got a boost up thinking about the possibility of winning the big life changing prize money. So at the beginning when it came to the lottery we rose in vibration and **became excited** when we put it on and sure enough our high energy state ensured that we had a few wins.

Then after a while we realised that the big one wasn't coming or going to be so easy to win and we slid down the vibrations back to our 'normal' level. Our expectations of winning the lottery subsided and we slipped down in vibration back to our old more negatively oriented mindset.

The temporary boost of hope, excitement and eager anticipation was replaced with our old habitual negative expectations of disappointment, doubt, frustration and fear.

Our pre-programmed and in general predominately negative ideas about life along with the associated feelings came back into play, so the initial surge of success tapered off as we slid back down the vibrations.

Bear in mind the two methods you are about to read will work just as well for winning the lottery, just try them and see how suddenly you are winning again.

It's all governed by the same thing, your level of belief.

Chapter 6

The Methods

My approach would be don't think too much about the race or your selection. Forget all the analysing and intense working out which horse has the best chance for all of the usual reasons, trainer, weight, form, conditions etc.

No need to worry about all of that because they all win and what you are really picking is the race that you will experience. When you get into the technicalities of the race you open the door for negative energy to come flooding in, too much to think about, too much to analyse, too many avenues to consider.

Keep it simple, make your choice and believe it has already won.

Allowing yourself to make judgments about everything leaves many avenues open for negative energy to enter the equation and this can then easily cause you to drift down from the higher vibrations to a vibrational place where your chances of winning lessen.

Your approach should be, you don't care if you lose. It does not affect your vibration in a negative way if you lose. You are detached from the outcome and this is what you must train yourself to feel, **nothing.** You hold your serenity, inner peace and joyous disposition no matter what.

This art of detachment helps to keep negativity out and that keeps your vibration as high as possible. Practice this and you will soon master the art of holding yourself in the high zone when betting on the horses, which will increase your chances of winning.

You must train yourself to use your mind in this way so don't get disillusioned if it takes a little time, remember practice makes perfect. As you prepare to make your choice for the race its best if you concentrate on feeling calm, serene and peaceful or going for the more active approach of excitement, joy and fun.

Either way you will be holding yourself in the higher vibrations where you have much more chance of bringing your choice home as the winner. Play around with this to see what approach suits you best.

The 3 Steps

The first method is a three step process that you can use to get yourself into the mindset of believing that your horse has already won the race.

1. **PREPARE:** It would be beneficial on a day that you are going to bet if you prepared yourself in the correct way and that means doing anything that helps **relax and calm** you. Such as going for a walk in nature, having a relaxing radox bath, going to the gym, meditating, walking the dog, watching uplifting TV programmes, listening to relaxing music, visualising a calm and relaxing scene. Whatever works for you will help because this raises your vibration and puts you in a much better feeling place to then be able to attain the **BELIEF** that your horse has won the race. The importance of this part of the process can't be overlooked, it is essential that you are in as high a vibration as possible for you to bring the result of your choice into your reality. In fact if you are not in the right 'mood' it may be wise to leave it for that day and wait for another time when you are. Even having a niggly little cold or feeling slightly under the weather for any reason can play havoc with your

ability to raise your vibration. So be aware of your general feeling of well being and factor this into the equation. I always spend 10 minutes visualising myself in a rowing boat on a calm peaceful lake to get my vibration as high as possible (as per step 3) before I attempt to enter into the belief that my horse has won and I find this works really well.

2. **SEE IT:** When you have chosen your horse and just before the race, I want you to find somewhere quiet where you can relax then close your eyes and run through a mini movie of what is going to happen. Remember it's all about the **feelings**. It's the **feelings** that will bring this into your reality.

See your horse just off the pace but perfectly placed as they approach the final furlong. Then he makes his move and surges past the other runners on the run in, drawing away from the field winning in great style with the jockey up in the saddle waving to the cheering crowd.

Then picture yourself laughing and throwing up bundles of money into the air and then spraying champagne over the crowd as you celebrate your fantastic win. See the look on your

face of sheer joy and see yourself laughing as you make the most of the moment. (Bask in the **feelings** and let them wash over you, really feel it).
BELIEVE IT...FEEL IT

3. **FEEL IT:** When the race actually starts keep running over in your mind the mini movie of your horse surging away from the field and crossing the finish line and keep repeating over and over in your mind *(the name of your horse) wins the race ahead of the field for an amazing victory.*
BELIEVE IT...FEEL IT

When you are doing this there is no need for stress or too much intense effort as it all works better if you do it in a light, carefree, easy sort of way. Remember win or lose you are happy, calm and chilled out.

Another way that you can do **Step 3** is to get yourself out of the way (energy wise) because when you are caught up in the high energy approach and are actively holding your energy up, it's possible that you might unknowingly allow in negative energy through a shimmer of anxiety and this can happen occasionally especially when you first start doing it.

I actually like the getting out of the way option and all I do is, when the race starts I imagine myself in a rowing boat floating on a calm beautiful lake. I still run through the mini movie of my horse winning a couple of times but then I let it go and concentrate on keeping my energy totally serene.

I picture myself laying back in the boat focussing on keeping the water perfectly still no matter what is happening in the race. Total peace is my focus with absolutely still water all around me not a ripple upon the surface. I hold this feeling of tranquillity throughout the race and basically give the race no energy whatsoever, no matter what is happening.

Absolute stillness is my goal even if my horse is nowhere to be seen because then it becomes a valuable exercise in energy control. Holding the feeling of inner peace keeps me in the higher vibrations and that ensures my earlier visualisation of winning is not compromised.

So instead of trying to hold the feelings of having won the race after my initial visualisation I am letting it all go and basking in serenity and allowing my vision of having won to unfold.

I find this works just as well and you can try the high energy approach (forcing yourself to hold the feeling of excitement during the race) or the serenity approach (letting it all go) to see what suits you best.

Maybe bounce between the two when you find your control wavering in one of them, it's always good to have another option to try.

After a while you will be able to use the three step mcthod with either of the Step 3 options in any environment, such as in the betting shop or at the races by tweaking the process slightly to suit your surroundings.

You can become proficient in any given situation. All it takes is practice and as you notice something **amazing is really happening** you will gain more and more confidence in the process.

It's important to remember you need to practice this, as in any skill practice makes perfect, so don't get disillusioned if at first you feel it's not working well enough, keep at it and you will soon see results.

It's when you start getting results that you will gain more and more confidence and it will get easier and easier.

Nobody picks up a golf club for the first time and hits the ball perfectly every time, it takes practice and dedication to hone your skills and this is no different.

Maybe keep a record of your bets to see how you do over a period of time when you are trying out the methods as opposed to when you are not using them and compare the difference.

And you don't have to put money on when you are just trying it out concentrate on building belief in the system first.

Thank you for reading my book and 'good luck' or should I say **'Just Believe'** because as you know, **this is the secret.**

Feedback

Please feel free to let me know of the success you have using the methods or if you have any comments or questions about anything else.

And if you have any requests for future titles in 'The Real Secret' series of books please let me know.

Also if you would be so kind as to leave a review for this book on Amazon I would be very grateful.

I can be contacted on email:
stevewharton23@aol.co.uk

Thank you

Steve

Reference:

Recommended Books

Feeling is the Secret

By Neville Goddard

The Law of Asumption

By Neville Goddard

Imagination Creates Reality

By Neville Goddard

Your Faith is your fortune

By Neville Goddard

Ask and It Is Given

By Esther Hicks and Jerry Hicks

Think and Grow Rich

By Napoleon Hill

The Power of Positive Thinking

By Norman Vincent Peale

The Magic of Believing

By Claude Bristol

The Power of your subconscious mind

By Joseph Murphy

The Power of Intention

By Dr Wayne Dyer

Change Your Thoughts, Change Your Life

By Dr Wayne Dyer

High Vibrational Thinking
The power to change your life

By Steve Wharton

This Book WILL Change Your Life

By Steve Wharton

The Secret

By Rhonda Byrne

The Monk who sold his Ferrari

By Robin Sharma

Quantum Physics

Some interesting leads you can follow if you want to know more about the leading thought on Parallel Realities. (Where other horses win the race).

Space.com

Some researchers base their ideas of parallel universes on quantum mechanics, the mathematical description of subatomic particles. In quantum mechanics, multiple states of existence for tiny particles are all possible at the same time — a "wave function" encapsulates all of those possibilities.

However, when we actually look, we only ever observe one of the possibilities.

According to the Copenhagen interpretation of quantum mechanics as described by the **Stanford Encyclopedia of Philosophy**, we observe an outcome when the wave function "collapses" into a single reality.

But the many-worlds theory proposes instead that every time one state, or outcome, is observed, there is another "world" in which a different quantum outcome becomes reality.

This is a branching arrangement, in which instant by instant, our perceived universe branches into near-infinite alternatives.

Those alternate universes are completely separate and unable to intersect, so while there may be uncountable versions of you living a life that's slightly — or wildly — different from your life in this world, you'd never know it.

https://www.space.com/32728-parallel-universes.html

Forbes.com

For some of us, the idea of parallel Universes sparks our wildest dreams. If there are other Universes where certain events had different outcomes — where just one crucial decision went a different way — perhaps there could be some way to access them.

Perhaps particles, fields, or even people could be transported from one to the other, enabling us to live in a Universe that's better, in some ways, than our own.

These ideas have a foothold in theoretical physics as well, from the myriad of possible outcomes from quantum mechanics as well as ideas of the multiverse. But do they have anything to do with observable, measurable reality?

Recently, **a claim has surfaced** asserting that **we've found evidence for parallel Universes**, and Jordan Colby Cox wants to know what it means, asking:

https://www.forbes.com/sites/startswithaba
ng/2020/05/22/ask-ethan-have-we-finally-
found-evidence-for-a-parallel-
universe/?sh=6ca43c7a42fc

npr.org

Our universe might be really, really big — but finite. Or it might be infinitely big. Both cases, says physicist Brian Greene, are possibilities, but if the latter is true, so is another posit: There are only so many ways matter can arrange itself within that infinite universe. Eventually, matter has to repeat itself and arrange itself in similar ways. So if the universe is infinitely large, it is also home to infinite parallel universes.

Does that sound confusing? Try this:

Think of the universe like a deck of cards. "Now, if you shuffle that deck, there's just so many orderings that can happen," Greene says. "If you shuffle that deck enough times, the orders will have to repeat. Similarly, with an infinite universe and only a finite number of complexions of matter, the way in which matter arranges itself has to repeat."

Greene, the author of *The Elegant Universe* and *The Fabric of the Cosmos*, tackles the existence of multiple universes in his latest book, *The Hidden Reality: Parallel Universes and the Deep Laws of the Cosmos*.
https://www.npr.org/2011/01/24/1329322
68/a-physicist-explains-why-parallel-
universes-may-exist

Forthcoming Titles

The Real Secret to improving your Business

The Real Secret to Great Relationships

The Real Secret to Winning the Lottery

The Real Secret to Perfect Putting

The Real Secret to Creating your Reality

The Real Secret to Defeating Bullies

The Real Secret to Overcoming Depression

The Real Secret to getting promoted

The Real Secret to attracting wealth

The Real Secret to super confidence

The Real Secret to becoming successful

The Real Secret to peak performance

The Real Secret to beating anxiety

Printed in Great Britain
by Amazon

23128018R00036